SPELLING

YEAR 5

PASCAL PRESS

Reading Eggspress Spelling Workbook – Year 5

Reprinted 2016, 2020, 2021, 2022, 2026

ISBN: 978-1-74215-310-0

Distrbuted by:
Pascal Press
PO Box 250
Glebe NSW 2037

Ph: (02) 8585 4085
Fax: (02) 8585 4058

Email: info@blake.com.au
Website: www.blake.com.au

Publisher: Katy Pike
Series editor: Amy Russo
Editors: Laura Anderson, Stacey Belgre
Designed and typeset by The Modern Art Production Group
Printed in China by 1010 Printing International Ltd

CONTENTS

WHAT IS READING EGGSPRESS?

Reading Eggspress is an online program designed to build language and literacy skills for students in Years 1–6. The program has targeted lesson sequences for Comprehension and Spelling that align with national curriculum standards for achievement. With built-in rewards, access to over 3500 e-books and rich assessment data to track progress, the Reading Eggspress program individualises learning to help students achieve their personal best.

How does the Reading Eggspress Spelling Program work?

Research proves that students have more spelling success if they learn to recognise common spelling patterns and generalisations as part of an explicit and systematic teaching program. The *Reading Eggspress Spelling program* focuses on common spelling rules, generalisations and strategies using a combination of teaching videos, engaging online activities, games and tests with fully integrated student books.

The *Reading Eggspress Spelling books* for Years 1–6 extend students as they learn, use and apply their spelling skills across a range of written activities. The student books work alongside the online program to reinforce learning for each lesson.

The *Reading Eggspress Spelling program* is structured to provide instruction on a spelling rule, strategy or generalisation with 36 lessons per year level. Each lesson is centred on a carefully crafted word list, based around the sound, structure or meaning features of words. These word lists have been created by consulting educational research and the Australian Curriculum.

Self-paced systematic program

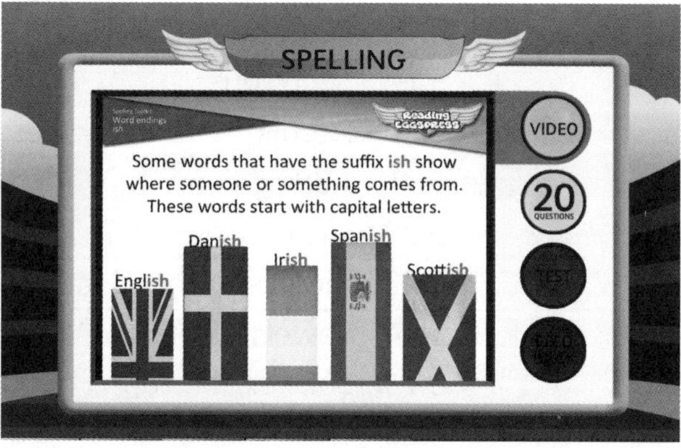

Easy to understand videos

Assessment and instant feedback

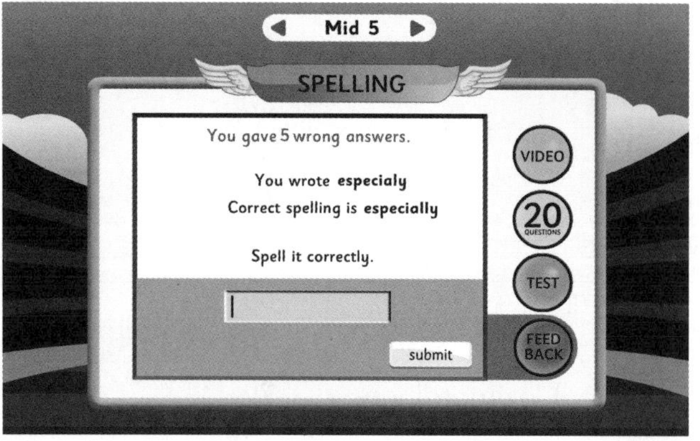

Practice activities

Reading Eggspress Spelling and the Australian Curriculum

Each lesson focuses on a core set of 20 words and 10 challenge words to extend students. These lists have been created to align with the Australian Curriculum Content Descriptions and Elaborations.

Year 5 Language

Language variation and change
ACELA1500

Understand that the pronunciation, spelling and meanings of words have histories and change over time

- recognising that a knowledge of word origins is not only interesting in its own right, but that it extends students' knowledge of vocabulary and spelling
- exploring examples of words in which pronunciation, writing and meaning has changed over time, including words from a range of cultures

Expressing and developing ideas
ACELA1513

Understand how to use banks of known words, as well as word origins, prefixes and suffixes, to learn and spell new words

ACELA1514

Recognise uncommon plurals, for example 'foci'

- using knowledge of word origins and roots and related words to interpret and spell unfamiliar words, and learning about how these roots impact on plurals

Reading Eggspress Spelling

Each lesson uses a combination of activities from the following categories:

Proofreading: self-directed checking of written text. Proofreading assists the development of reading and writing.

Visual memory: the Look-say-cover-write-check creates a visual memory of the word. It is important as a self-correction skill.

Definitions: morphemic understanding of words. This skill is used selectively where an understanding of the etymology and morphological structure benefits orthographic understanding.

Word families: groups of words that share common morphemes. Identifying visual and morphemic commonalities aids accurate spelling and is used throughout the program.

Word sorts: groups of words that share a common theme. Word sorts have been integrated as grouping together like ideas helps learners make sense of the world around them.

Overview of Spelling Aspects Covered in Year 5

Spelling Aspect	Areas Covered	Pages
Digraphs and trigraphs	oo, ou; wh, ph, gh	56, 57, 58, 59
Endings	rse, rce; ent, ant; and, end, ond; our, ure; ish; age, idge; ence, ance	4, 5, 6, 7, 8, 9, 14, 15, 28, 29, 44, 45, 60, 61
Prefixes	un, dis, mis; anti, circum, extra, semi	30, 31, 72, 73
Suffixes	fy; ic; ity; ive; s, es; ist; ous; ment, ship, hood, dom; ion, ian; ly	10, 11, 16, 17, 20, 21, 26, 27, 32, 33, 34, 35, 38, 39, 40, 41, 46, 47, 50, 51, 64, 65
Letter patterns	adding to fer; ch; que	42, 43, 52, 53, 66, 67
Origins	Latin	24, 25
Other aspects of spelling	vowel exceptions; homophones; silent letters; compound words; portmanteau words; palindromes; vowels; tricky words; eponyms; word building; loan words	2, 3, 12, 13, 18,19, 22, 23, 36, 37, 48, 49, 54, 55, 62, 63, 68, 69, 70, 71

MY PROGRESS CHART • LESSONS 5.1 – 5.18

Name ____________________

Lesson	Level	Online test score	Pages	Self-assessment *With this list I feel ...*
5.1 Vowel exceptions		/10	2 - 3	
5.2 Endings: rse, rce		/10	4 - 5	
5.3 Endings: ent, ant		/10	6 - 7	
5.4 and, end, ond		/10	8 - 9	
5.5 Suffix: fy		/10	10 - 11	
5.6 Homophones		/10	12 - 13	
5.7 Endings: our, ure		/10	14 - 15	
5.8 Suffix: ic		/10	16 - 17	
5.9 Silent letters		/10	18 - 19	
5.10 Suffix: ity		/10	20 - 21	
5.11 Compound words		/10	22 - 23	
5.12 Latin origins		/10	24 - 25	
5.13 Suffix: ive		/10	26 - 27	
5.14 Ending: ish		/10	28 - 29	
5.15 un, dis, mis		/10	30 - 31	
5.16 Plurals		/10	32 - 33	
5.17 Suffix: ist		/10	34 - 35	
5.18 Portmanteau words		/10	36 - 37	

MY PROGRESS CHART • LESSONS 5.19 – 5.36

Name ______________________________

Lesson	Level	Online test score	Pages	Self-assessment *With this list I feel ...*
5.19 Suffix: ous		/10	38 - 39	
5.20 Plurals		/10	40 - 41	
5.21 Adding to fer		/10	42 - 43	
5.22 Endings: age, idge		/10	44 - 45	
5.23 ment, ship, hood		/10	46 - 47	
5.24 Vowels		/10	48 - 49	
5.25 Suffixes: ion, ian		/10	50 - 51	
5.26 ch		/10	52 - 53	
5.27 Tricky words		/10	54 - 55	
5.28 oo, ou		/10	56 - 57	
5.29 wh, ph, gh		/10	58 - 59	
5.30 ence, ance		/10	60 - 61	
5.31 Eponyms		/10	62 - 63	
5.32 Suffix: ly		/10	64 - 65	
5.33 que		/10	66 - 67	
5.34 Word building		/10	68 - 69	
5.35 Loan words		/10	70 - 71	
5.36 anti, circum, extra		/10	72 - 73	

Vowel sounds – exceptions

List **1 Write the word.**

deaf ____
head ____
said ____
idea ____
meant ____
four ____
bread ____
mould ____
thread ____
great ____
famous ____
wealth ____
cousin ____
nourish ____
really ____
break ____
favour ____
dread ____
already ____
heavy ____

2 Sort the words.

Words with *ea*

____ ____
____ ____
____ ____
____ ____
____ ____
____ ____
____ ____

Words with *ou*

____ ____
____ ____
____ ____

3 Fill in the missing letter.

___eal___ ___ br___ ___d
wea___ ___h co___ s___n
___r___ak n___ ___ r___sh
f___m___ ___s d___ ___f
a___re___ ___y g___ ___ ___t

4 Name.

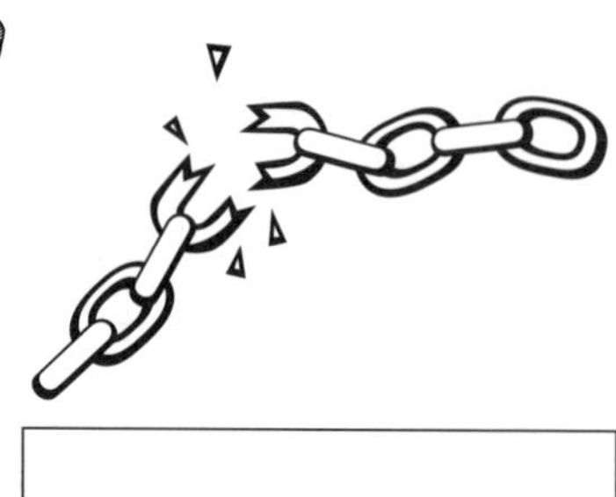

Vowel sounds – exceptions

5 Underline the spelling mistake. Write the word correctly.

We placed the clay in the mold ready to bake. ________

The chocolate mud cake was very hevy to eat. ________

Our pet dog was old and def. ________

Watching movies was a great ideea. ________

There were fore cupcakes left over. ________

Throughout his life he had saved all of his welth. ________

He sed he would be home for dinner. ________

Dad patted me on the hed as he walked past. ________

Mum asked me to cook dinner as a favor to her. ________

I carefully put the thred through the eye of the needle. ________

Challenge words

6 Write the word.

deadly ________

dreamt ________

heaven ________

meadow ________

couple ________

aisle ________

haiku ________

humour ________

trouble ________

boulder ________

7 Word clues. Which challenge word matches?

open field of grass ________

Japanese poem ________

funny ________

source of difficulty ________

fatal ________

large rock ________

imagined ________

corridor ________

two people ________

paradise ________

8 Another way to say it. Which challenge word could replace the underlined word/s?

The spider was <u>lethal</u>, if it bit you. ________

He walked hurriedly down the supermarket <u>lane</u> looking for rice. ________

They lifted the <u>large rock</u> with a crane. ________

She <u>fantasised</u> about a beach holiday, as the weather was cold. ________

Not everyone enjoyed Simon's <u>wit</u>. ________

They saw a <u>pair</u> of kangaroos in the paddock. ________

Word endings – rse, rce

List **1 Write the word.**

horse ____________________
worse ____________________
purse ____________________
verse ____________________
force ____________________
scarce ____________________
fierce ____________________
reverse ____________________
sparse ____________________
adverse ____________________
course ____________________
diverse ____________________
source ____________________
converse ____________________
immerse ____________________
averse ____________________
terse ____________________
divorce ____________________
resource ____________________
pierce ____________________

2 Sort the words.

Words that end in *rse*

________________ ________________
________________ ________________
________________ ________________
________________ ________________
________________ ________________
________________ ________________
________________ ________________

Words that end in *rce*

________________ ________________
________________ ________________
________________ ________________
________________ ________________

3 Complete these words with *rse* or *rce*.

reve____________ divo____________
dive____________ sou____________
imme____________ spa____________
pu____________ fie____________
resou____________ ve____________

4 Complete each sentence with a list word.

She rode her ________________ daily on the farm.
The shark looked ________________ with its toothy grin.
I read a ________________ from a poem at assembly.
The rain had been ________________ , so the crops were struggling.
I like to ________________ with my friends on the phone.
My dad has an ________________ reaction to peanuts.
I will ________________ myself to get up earlier tomorrow morning.
The mess in my room is ________________ today than it was yesterday.

Word endings – rse, rce

5 Meaning. Which list word means?

where something begins ______
to prick or break ______
in short supply ______
strength or effort ______
to completely cover in liquid ______
of different kinds or sorts ______

Challenge words

6 Write the word.

coarse ______
rehearse ______
traverse ______
reimburse ______
intersperse ______
coerce ______
disperse ______
commerce ______
enforce ______
reinforce ______

7 Word clues. Which challenge word matches?

cover or cross ______
scatter ______
rough ______
persuade ______
trade ______
add strength ______

8 Hidden words. Find the challenge word.

herrehearseqreh ______
foreenenforcecefo ______
reimreimburseurse ______
erserreinforceres ______

9 Another way to say it. Which challenge word could replace the underlined word/s?

Dad bought me the skateboard and I will <u>pay</u> him later. ______
Sophie and her friends will <u>go through</u> the play tonight. ______
The fabric was <u>rough</u> and scratchy on her skin. ______
Her brother would <u>pressure</u> her into doing his chores for him. ______
They will <u>scatter</u> the seeds over the soil. ______
They <u>impose</u> the rules to keep the students safe. ______
The ship had to <u>cross</u> the rough seas. ______
Dad will <u>strengthen</u> the fence with more posts. ______

Word endings – ent, ant

List

tenant
rodent
instant
urgent
pendant
tyrant
fluent
entrant
violent
evident
assistant
serpent
elegant
applicant
ancient
significant
magnificent
radiant
apparent
opponent

1 Write the word.

2 Sort the words.

ent

ant

3 Complete these words with *ent* or *ant*.

eleg_____	urg_____
radi_____	tyr_____
magnific_____	entr_____
viol_____	evid_____
ten_____	serp_____
applic_____	signific_____

4 Underline the spelling mistake. Write the word correctly.

The serpant slithered over the hot ground.

The aincient ruins were being preserved for future generations.

Guinea pigs are a type of rodant.

My mum's assistent answered her phone when I rang.

She wore a pretty silver pendent.

I didn't like the movie as it was very vilent.

My brother was going to be my opponant in the tennis tournament.

Word endings – ent, ant

5 Meaning. Which list word means?

a bully ______________
bright and shining ______________
obvious ______________
very old ______________
grand ______________
important ______________
brutal ______________
enemy ______________
a snake ______________
helper ______________
able to speak easily ______________
a small mammal ______________

Challenge words

6 Write the word.

warrant ______________
turbulent ______________
inhabitant ______________
instrument ______________
participant ______________
equivalent ______________
persistent ______________
extravagant ______________
nutrient ______________
adamant ______________

7 Word clues. Which challenge word matches?

resident ______________
determined ______________
equal to ______________
excessive ______________
rough ______________
player ______________

8 Hidden words. Find the challenge word.

prohwarrantent ______________
qtinstrumentmant ______________
extrnutrientant ______________
nuextravagantent ______________

9 Complete the sentence.

Bananas are a good source of the ______________ potassium.
Sam will be a ______________ in the running race.
The ocean was ______________ due to the rough wind.
The policeman had a ______________ for his arrest.
Her ______________ parents spoiled her with a magnificent jumping castle.
My favourite musical ______________ is the flute.
He is an ______________ of Australia.
She was ______________ in her swimming training.

Word endings – and, end, ond

List

second
legend
husband
depend
intend
beyond
pretend
defend
island
thousand
garland
amend
almond
diamond
suspend
descend
command
attend
offend
demand

1 Write the word.

2 Sort the words.

and

end

ond

3 Complete the words with *and, end* or *ond*.

sec____	garl____
husb____	alm____
int____	susp____
pret____	comm____
dem____	off____

4 Word clues. Which list word matches?

a precious jewel	a type of nut
the man a person is married to	to move downwards
to make-believe	to protect from harm
land surrounded by water	chain or wreath made of flowers

Word endings – and, end, ond

5 Meaning. Which list word means?

number equal to ten times one hundred ____________

to act falsely or to make believe ____________

to be present at ____________

to hang from a higher position ____________

to trust or rely on ____________

to tell forcefully or to order ____________

Challenge words

6 Write the word.

errand ____________

reprimand ____________

reverend ____________

reprehend ____________

Holland ____________

correspond ____________

commend ____________

comprehend ____________

apprehend ____________

vagabond ____________

7 Hidden words. Find the challenge word.

auiderrandiyub ____________

iaydcommenduajb ____________

ausbvagabondoiyn ____________

asccorrespondaoish ____________

asinreverendopaih ____________

asdjcomprehendoauib ____________

8 Word clues. Which challenge word matches?

chide ____________

capture ____________

communicate ____________

9 Another way to say it. Which challenge word could replace the underlined word/s?

The policewoman will <u>capture</u> the criminal. ____________

I will teach my dog to <u>understand</u> sit, beg and roll. ____________

Mum will <u>admonish</u> me for being late. ____________

My brother received a <u>scolding</u> for his messy room. ____________

Amsterdam is a city in <u>the Netherlands</u>. ____________

Everyone will <u>compliment</u> his brilliant assignment. ____________

His story will <u>match</u> with hers. ____________

The <u>vagrant</u> slept in the park at night. ____________

Word endings – fy

List **1 Write the word.**

verify ______
amplify ______
satisfy ______
glorify ______
gratify ______
justify ______
qualify ______
notify ______
signify ______
modify ______
classify ______
horrify ______
simplify ______
mystify ______
terrify ______
magnify ______
identify ______
beautify ______
certify ______
liquefy ______

2 Complete these list words.

sim ______ gra ______
cla ______ jus ______
amp ______ sig ______
liq ______ bea ______
ide ______ mys ______

3 Put the syllables back together.

fy-sa-tis ______
ue-liq-fy ______
fy-i-mod ______
ri-fy-ter ______
mys-fy-ti ______
pli-fy-sim ______
ni-sig-fy ______
i-grat-fy ______
ti-fy-jus ______
fy-no-ti ______
ni-mag-fy ______
ti-cer-fy ______

4 Underline the spelling mistake. Write the word correctly.

The speakers will amplifie the sound in the auditorium. ______
We will magnyfy the ant to see it better. ______
We had to notefy everyone of the new starting time. ______
The mess in my room will horify my mother! ______
We added some fresh flowers to bewtify the room. ______
We could identifie the food by the delicious smell. ______
I like to classifie my clothes by colours. ______
I tried to justifie why I should be allowed to stay up later. ______

Word endings – fy

5 Meaning. Which list word means?

to recognise ____________

to make sure something is true ____________

to tell about ____________

to praise, honour or worship ____________

to make something appear larger ____________

to endorse or guarantee ____________

Challenge words

6 Write the word.

specify ____________

pacify ____________

unify ____________

crucify ____________

rectify ____________

intensify ____________

dignify ____________

personify ____________

electrify ____________

diversify ____________

7 Word Clues. Which challenge word matches?

to give honour or prestige ____________

to shock ____________

to indicate explicitly ____________

to bring together ____________

give human characteristics to something ____________

8 Hidden words. Find the challenge word.

cruscrucifyaosu ____________

sifydiversifyasug ____________

divepacifypac ____________

aiysrectifysiyu ____________

9 Complete the sentence.

We will ____________ the flowers in our creative writing.

Her amazing performance will ____________ the audience.

The dummy worked to ____________ the baby.

I will ____________ to situation by explaining the mistake.

The farmer plans to ____________ the crops he grows.

I will ____________ the colour jumper I would like.

The hard times spent together would ____________ the family.

I will not ____________ your accusation with a response!

Homophones

List **1 Write the word.**

peace ______
piece ______
guest ______
guessed ______
past ______
passed ______
you ______
ewe ______
horde ______
hoard ______
sweet ______
suite ______
wary ______
weary ______
cue ______
queue ______
bridle ______
bridal ______
patients ______
patience ______

2 Fill in the correct list words.

The ______ had correctly ______ where his bedroom was. (guessed, guest)

The chocolates in the hotel ______ are ______ and delicious. (sweet, suite)

We halved the ______ of cake to keep the ______ between the two siblings. (peace, piece)

There was a ______ of people trying to find the ______ of old coins. (hoard, horde)

3 Unscramble these list words.

oyu	______	dohre	______
iepce	______	uce	______
spadse	______	etius	______
rwya	______	rdibla	______
intspate	______	uesdegs	______

4 Underline the spelling mistake. Write the word correctly.

My grandparents horde old newspapers dating back to 1975. ______
We walked right passed the store. ______
The horse whinnied as his bridal was too tight. ______
The guessed arrived at the hotel too early to check in. ______
The group was working towards world piece. ______
The you bleated loudly as we walked through the field. ______
The chocolate brownie was suite and moist. ______
We were wary after our long hike in the bush. ______

Homophones

5 Missing syllable.

Write the missing syllable.

________-tience

pa-________

________-dle

________-al

war-________

6 Name.

Challenge words

7 Write the word.

morning ____________

mourning ____________

principle ____________

principal ____________

weather ____________

whether ____________

compliment ____________

complement ____________

stationary ____________

stationery ____________

8 Word Clues. Which challenge word matches?

to praise ____________

climate ____________

dawn ____________

static ____________

a belief ____________

pen and paper ____________

9 Hidden words. Find the challenge word.

ourmorningingn ____________

whewhethermou ____________

cipaprincipalprin ____________

compcomplimentime ____________

10 Complete the sentence.

We are unsure ____________ the ____________ will be sunny tomorrow.

The customer gave the chef a ____________ on his ability to ____________ his meal with good service.

We didn't know that in the ____________ we would be ____________ the loss of our pet.

The ____________ cupboard remained ____________ in the office.

The ____________ would not allow the students to bring mobiles to school on ____________ .

Word endings – our, ure

List 1 Write the word.

vapour ______
culture ______
armour ______
flavour ______
pasture ______
clamour ______
texture ______
future ______
lecture ______
figure ______
valour ______
nurture ______
rigour ______
furniture ______
sculpture ______
leisure ______
tumour ______
moisture ______
creature ______
torture ______

2 Sort the words.

Words that end in *our*

______ ______
______ ______
______ ______
______ ______

Words that end in *ure*

______ ______
______ ______
______ ______
______ ______
______ ______
______ ______
______ ______

3 Fill in the missing letters.

fur___it___ ___ ___ l___ ___s___re
p___ ___tu___ ___ t___mo___ ___
m___ ___st___ ___e ___a___ou___
___ ___rtu___ ___ ar___ ___u___

4 Name.

______ ______ ______ ______

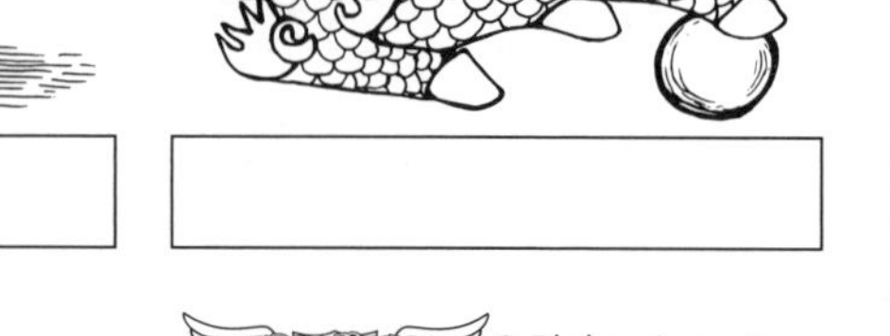

Word endings – our, ure

5 Complete each sentence with a list word.

The __________________ of the rock was rough and scratchy.
The __________________ on the ground showed that it had been raining.
Reading was her favourite __________________ activity.
She saved money so that in the __________________ she could buy a computer.
Strawberry is her favourite __________________ of milkshake.
My dad received a medal of __________________ for his bravery in the war.
They enforced the new law with great __________________ .
They are carving a __________________ for the exhibition out of stone.
The __________________ skaters practised their routine daily.
For a tiny __________________, the cicada certainly makes a lot of noise!

Challenge words

6 Write the word.

departure __________________
signature __________________
fervour __________________
neighbour __________________
composure __________________
rupture __________________
exposure __________________
temperature __________________
agriculture __________________
miniature __________________

7 Word Clues. Which challenge word matches?

autograph __________________
fever __________________
horticulture __________________
leaving __________________
tiny __________________
person next door __________________

8 Hidden words. Find the challenge words.

sureexposureexp __________________
vorffervourvofe __________________
surocomposureco __________________
rappruptureure __________________

9 Another way to say it. Which challenge word could replace the underlined word?

The <u>break</u> in the dam wall caused a flood. __________________
Diana kept her <u>self-control</u> during the ordeal. __________________
The reporter wrote about the <u>unveiling</u> of underworld crime. __________________

Suffixes – ic

List **1 Write the word.**

music ______
poetic ______
magic ______
topic ______
plastic ______
basic ______
artistic ______
public ______
tonic ______
magnetic ______
heroic ______
romantic ______
dramatic ______
angelic ______
specific ______
symbolic ______
historic ______
fantastic ______
academic ______
horrific ______

2 Complete the sentence with a list word.

She plays beautiful ______ on the piano.

If it's not private, it's ______.

The old building is of ______ importance.

My photos aren't that good as my camera is pretty ______.

Something that has the power to attract things is ______.

A dove is ______ of peace.

He chose an interesting ______ for his speech.

The juice is in a ______ bottle.

3 Fill in the missing syllables.

po-et-______
______-a-dem-______
an-______-ic
______-tas-tic
mag-______
hor-rif-______
ar-______-______
ton-______
ro-______-tic
he-______-______

4 Write the list words in alphabetical order.

Suffixes – ic

5 Meaning. Which list word means?

noble and courageous ________________

having to do with school ________________

sound with tones and rhythms that can be listened to and enjoyed ________________

a medicine that brings back one's strength ________________

out of the ordinary and exciting ________________

showing skill in creating ________________

Challenge words

6 Write the word.

realistic ________________

mechanic ________________

strategic ________________

optimistic ________________

automatic ________________

enthusiastic ________________

scientific ________________

sympathetic ________________

democratic ________________

photographic ________________

7 Hidden words. Find the challenge word.

tomioptimisticoasui ________________

phophotographicashb ________________

enthenthusiasticaoisn ________________

asunsympatheticiyuna ________________

istirealisticreal ________________

ficscientificscui ________________

cratdemocraticdemo ________________

memmechanicmecin ________________

matautomaticauto ________________

egicstrategicstrat ________________

8 Complete the sentence. Which challenge word matches?

The ________________ experiment taught them how plants grew.

It was a ________________ move to keep their best swimmer until last.

The ________________ doors opened as we entered the hospital.

He brought his camera and other ________________ equipment.

The ________________ repaired our car.

She was very ________________ about her chances.

He was kind and ________________ to his sad friend.

The election to appoint a new leader was very ________________.

Silent letters

List **1 Write the word.**

debt ______
doubt ______
lamb ______
sandwich ______
autumn ______
solemn ______
column ______
soften ______
answer ______
whose ______
subtle ______
succumb ______
muscle ______
fascinate ______
crescent ______
Wednesday ______
rhyme ______
thistle ______
whistle ______
moisten ______

2 Circle the silent letters in each word.

sandwich	solemn
subtle	fascinate
debt	whistle
whose	rhyme
moisten	thistle
autumn	column
lamb	muscle
answer	Wednesday
doubt	crescent
soften	succumb

3 Unscramble these list words.

ensmol	______	utbdo	______
sletiht	______	sctrcnee	______
csbmucu	______	netsiom	______
ftsnoe	______	ebtd	______
hsowe	______	euslbt	______
wdanscih	______	tewshil	______
rewsna	______	elcsum	______

4 Underline the spelling mistake. Write the word correctly.

Wenesday is in the middle of the week. ______
My right leg musle hurt after I finished running. ______
I made a chicken and cheese sanwich for my lunch. ______
The leaves turn brown and fall off the trees in autum. ______
Thomas likes to wistle as he walks to school. ______
No words ryme with orange. ______
I wrote a funny colum for the school magazine. ______
The stories about the ancient pharaohs fasinate me. ______

5 Meaning. Which list word means?

to give in to; yield ____________

to make slightly wet ____________

to not know for sure ____________

to attract and hold the interest of ____________

serious in appearance or mood ____________

a kind of plant with purple flowers ____________

Challenge words

6 Write the word.

abscess ____________

assignment ____________

campaign ____________

foreign ____________

government ____________

psychology ____________

pneumonia ____________

receipt ____________

raspberry ____________

mortgage ____________

7 Hidden words. Find the challenge word.

paiccampaignasihc ____________

asupnpneumoniaiys ____________

fgovgovernmentagov ____________

aiusgtreceiptaosug ____________

mortmortgagegage ____________

aseaassignmentaouyh ____________

8 Word clues. Which challenge word matches?

task ____________

people in authority ____________

ulcer ____________

from overseas ____________

9 Complete the sentence.

He completed the ____________ and handed it to his teacher.

English was a ____________ language to the new French student.

The top she wore was the colour of a ____________.

He studied ____________ as he was interested in how the mind worked.

The shop assistant handed me a ____________ for my purchase.

The dentist told me the pain was caused by an ____________.

Suffixes – ity

List

electricity
reality
curiosity
publicity
ability
equality
clarity
intensity
normality
hostility
minority
security
identity
majority
mobility
continuity
brutality
prosperity
personality
maturity

1 Write the word.

2 Write the list words in alphabetical order.

3 Fill in the missing letters.

___ros___ ___ r___ ___ ___

m___b___li___ ___

h___sti___ ___ ___ ___

conti___ ___i___ ___

___i___orit___

pu___l___cit___

___lar___ ___ ___

r___ ___ l___ t ___

4 Complete each sentence with a list word.

His swimming ________________ has improved.

The ________________ of the workout made me sweaty and tired.

Solar panels make ________________ from light.

We lock our front door for ________________ when we aren't at home.

The ________________ of the class eat cereal for breakfast, with only a few eating toast.

She had a kind and happy ________________.

She watched the older children playing with growing ________________.

Suffixes – ity

5 Meaning. Which list word means?

having ease and flexibility of motion ________________

the power to do something ________________

the condition of being very cruel ________________

the true situation ________________

the state or condition of being pure or clear ________________

the attention someone gets from the media ________________

a stong desire to know or learn something ________________

Challenge words

6 Write the word.

possibility ________________

opportunity ________________

community ________________

simplicity ________________

necessity ________________

productivity ________________

uniformity ________________

sensitivity ________________

flexibility ________________

responsibility ________________

7 Hidden words. Find the challenge word.

proproductivityeti ________________

filflexibilityexib ________________

sennecessityess ________________

niuuniformitytiy ________________

sinsimplicityitie ________________

popopportunitytun ________________

enssensitivityive ________________

8 Word clues. Which challenge word matches?

a group of people ________________

all the same ________________

a chance ________________

9 Complete the sentence.

Looking after a pet is a big ________________.

The forecaster told us that rain was a ________________ for tomorrow.

Dancers do exercises to improve their ________________.

His room looked modern because of its ________________.

Food and water are a ________________ to human beings.

She has a ________________ to grass that makes her very itchy.

He had an ________________ to be on television.

Compound words

List **1 Write the word.**

deadline ____________
daybreak ____________
teammate ____________
highway ____________
goodbye ____________
warehouse ____________
background ____________
eyesight ____________
textbook ____________
watermelon ____________
cartwheel ____________
newsstand ____________
schoolwork ____________
spacewalk ____________
headache ____________
butterfingers ____________
timetable ____________
weeknight ____________
tablespoon ____________
skyscraper ____________

2 Fill in the missing part.

cart________	________walk
time________	________stand
good________	________way
butter________	________line
sky________	ware________
________spoon	water________
eye________	back________
________mate	________book
head________	________work
day________	week________

3 Fill in the missing syllables.

time-ta-________
________-ache
sky-________-er
but-________-fin-gers
ta-________-spoon
text-________
school-________
wa-________-mel-________

4 Word clues. Which list word matches?

something an astronaut would do ____________
a pain in the head ____________
the ability to see ____________
tasks your teacher gives you ____________
after dark from Monday to Friday ____________
saying farewell ____________
a member of your group ____________
the date by which something must be done ____________

Compound words

5 Name.

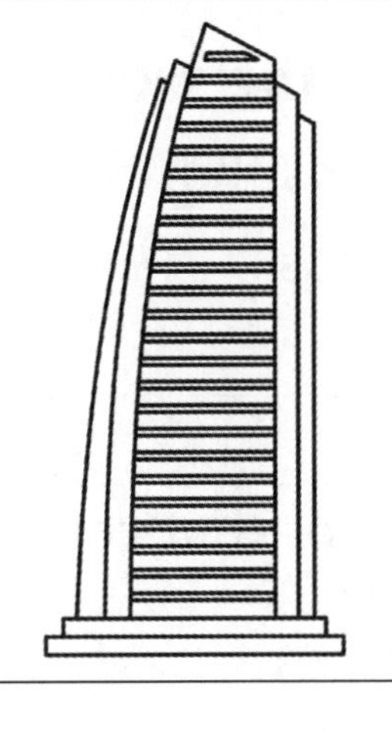

Challenge words

6 Write the word.

wastepaper ______
superhuman ______
roundabout ______
courthouse ______
earthbound ______
undercurrent ______
thunderbolt ______
bodyguard ______
candlelight ______
earthworm ______

7 Hidden words. Find the challenge word.

asrbodyguardaish ______
snugroundaboutasuh ______
lighcandlelightcanigh ______
ssefsuperhumanahanh ______
thththunderboltasina ______
papewastepaperzasu ______
asdundercurrentashn ______
eaeaearthwormasih ______
courtcourthousechou ______
oundearthboundearb ______

8 Another way to say it. Which challenge word could replace the underlined word/s?

The cars slowed down as they approached the <u>traffic circle</u>. ______
The judge delivered the sentence in the <u>tribunal</u>. ______
The man amazed everyone with his <u>extraordinary</u> strength. ______
We could sense the <u>feeling</u> of hostility in the room. ______
The celebrity's <u>minder</u> made sure that she arrived safely. ______
The <u>little animal</u> buried itself in the dirt. ______
She tore up the pages and put them in the <u>rubbish</u> basket. ______
A penguin is a <u>terrestrial</u> bird as it cannot fly. ______

Words with Latin origins

List **1 Write the word.**

literacy ______
habitat ______
benefit ______
inhabit ______
dome ______
literate ______
domestic ______
alien ______
domain ______
literal ______
aquatic ______
aquarium ______
habitable ______
habitation ______
inhabitant ______
aquaplane ______
feral ______
benign ______
aquanaut ______
literary ______

2 Sort the words.

Words that come from the Latin word *domus*

______ ______
______ ______

Words that come from the Latin word *aqua*

______ ______
______ ______

Words that come from the Latin word *bene*

______ ______

Words that come from the Latin word *habitare*

______ ______
______ ______
______ ______

Words that come from the Latin word *litera*

______ ______
______ ______

3 Underline the spelling mistake. Write the word correctly.

The doume above the stadium was very high. ______
The receptionist gave them a benine smile. ______
The main benifit of exercise is a healthy heart. ______
The monkeys' habbitat at the zoo mimicked the jungle. ______
Someone who can read and write is litirate. ______
The litral translation made more sense than the altered version. ______
The removal of mould made their house more habitabel. ______
The ferel cat looked hungry and dirty. ______

Words with Latin origins

4 Fill in the missing syllables.

a-quar-i-__________
__________-i-tat
lit-__________-a-cy
lit-er-__________-y
do-__________-tic
in-__________-it-ant
a-__________-en
aq-__________-plane
__________-ral
hab-it-a-__________

Challenge words

5 Write the word.

aquamarine __________
uninhabitable __________
alias __________
alibi __________
beneficial __________
beneficially __________
benefactor __________
ferocious __________
domestically __________
alliteration __________

6 Hidden words. Find the challenge word.

tasdaliasaseuy __________
ciousferociousaugs __________
sadrdomesticallyweiyh __________
asudhyalibiasdu __________
aquaaaquamarineuysh __________
fisibeneficiallylly __________

7 Word clues. Which challenge word matches?

fierce __________
favourable __________
blue-green __________
known by another name __________

8 Complete the sentence.

The hospital had a wing named after its main __________.
'Penny picked pretty petals' is an example of __________.
The water was a beautiful __________ colour.
He couldn't have committed the crime as he had an __________.
Eating many fruits is __________ to your health.
The desert wasteland was completely __________.
The shark looked __________ because it had so many teeth.
Her __________ was Princess Bananahammock.

Suffixes – ive

List **1 Write the word.**

active
captive
detective
extensive
creative
intensive
expensive
explosive
selective
objective
impulsive
secretive
attentive
formative
attractive
narrative
productive
massive
offensive
connective

2 Write the list words in alphabetical order.

3 Put the letters in the right order.

ect-conn-ive
ive-ob-ject
at-ive-cre
ret-ive-sec
sive-int-en
plos-ex-ive
tive-form-a
ive-ens-off
ive-uct-prod
sive-ten-ex

4 Word clues. Which list word matches?

busy, full of energy
something that looks good
something incredibly large
costing a lot of money
a person who follows clues to find the answer
a story
careful in choosing

Suffixes – ive

5 Meaning. Which list word means?

able to make something new or with imagination ______

causing anger or hurt feelings ______

acting without thinking or planning ______

held as a prisoner ______

something that connects things ______

a goal that a person works towards ______

Challenge words

6 Write the word.

sensitive ______

digestive ______

expressive ______

descriptive ______

repetitive ______

comparative ______

possessive ______

imaginative ______

competitive ______

excessive ______

7 Word clues. Which challenge word matches?

fanciful ______

detailed ______

not sharing ______

too much ______

easily hurt ______

ambitious ______

8 Hidden words. Find the challenge word.

petrepetitiveive ______

exivexcessivecess ______

tivedigestivedigi ______

9 Complete the sentence.

The boy wrote a ______ paragraph about his holiday.

The girl was very ______ and always wanted to win.

There was an ______ amount of food at the party.

The little boy had a very ______ face.

The song had a very catchy and ______ beat.

I was very ______ of my favourite toy.

Word endings – ish

List

English
nourish
sheepish
reddish
astonish
furnish
sluggish
cherish
childish
rubbish
varnish
stylish
establish
perish
vanquish
youngish
demolish
replenish
flourish
fiendish

1 Write the word.

2 Complete these list words.

sh ______
che ______
es ______
st ______
fi ______
En ______
fl ______
as ______

3 Unscramble these list words.

hpseri ______
ysthlis ______
espehhsi ______
lpenrihes ______
ifndseih ______
yhunogsi ______
aosinhts ______
hlsfuior ______
qvnuihas ______
hcishre ______

4 Complete each sentence with a list word.

They speak ______ as well as German in Germany.
He behaved in a ______ manner and got into trouble.
The sky had a ______ tinge from the bushfire.
They had to ______ the building as it was ruined.
Once the chair was sanded, they had to apply ______.
We eat food to ______ our bodies.
We always ______ a set of class rules at the beginning of the year.
There was a pile of smelly ______ on the side of the road.

5 In a group. Write the list word that belongs in each group.

young, younger, ______

child, childlike, ______

red, redder, ______

garbage, trash, ______

style, styles, ______

furniture, furnishings, ______

Challenge words

6 Write the word.

accomplish ______

anguish ______

distinguish ______

squeamish ______

extinguish ______

diminish ______

relinquish ______

feverish ______

embellish ______

amateurish ______

7 Hidden words. Find the challenge word.

squeesqueamishsque ______

fevefeverishsuiha ______

ameturamateurishamat ______

dimmdiminishiwha ______

llishembellishembel ______

accioaccomplishaccom ______

8 Word clues. Which challenge word matches?

achieve ______

burning up ______

grief ______

queasy ______

9 Another way to say it. Which challenge word could replace the underlined word/s?

The firefighter had to <u>put out</u> the flame using special foam. ______

The cooks were <u>inexperienced</u>, but were learning all the time. ______

It was hard to <u>differentiate</u> between the identical twins. ______

I will <u>adorn</u> my hat with sequins and glitter. ______

My sister wants to <u>quit</u> her role as swimming captain. ______

Speed limits help to <u>decrease</u> the number of accidents. ______

Prefixes – un, dis, mis

List **1 Write the word.**

unknown ______
unravel ______
mislead ______
dislocate ______
uncertain ______
disappear ______
unpleasant ______
dissolve ______
misplaced ______
misjudge ______
unfortunate ______
unusual ______
discourage ______
misconduct ______
miscalculate ______
unexpected ______
distasteful ______
unemployed ______
misguided ______
disapprove ______

2 Sort the words.

un

______ ______
______ ______
______ ______
______ ______

dis

______ ______
______ ______
______ ______

mis

______ ______
______ ______
______ ______

3 Word clues. Which list word matches?

melt ______
surprise ______
odd ______
vanish ______
unappetising ______
disentangle ______

4 Fill the missing letters

m___scon___u___t
___ ___stast___ ___ul
___ ___expect___ ___
d___ ___ap___ro___ ___
u___cer___ ___in

___nf___rt___na___e
d___st___s___ef___l
___ne___p___o___ ___d
m___s___ ___ad
u___ra___e___

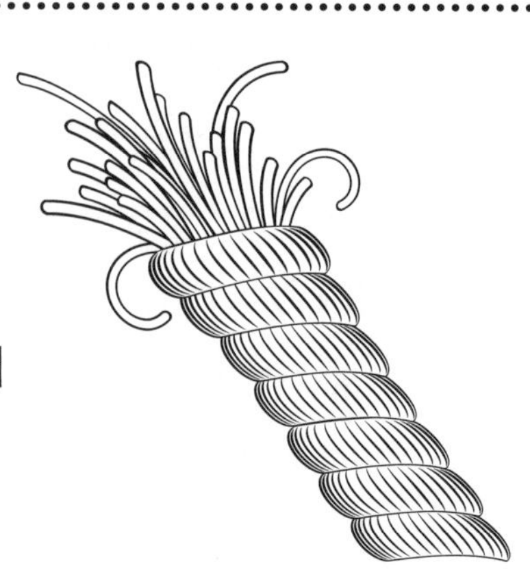

Prefixes – un, dis, mis

5 Underline the spelling mistake. Write the word correctly.

She can disapear so quietly that no one notices. ____________

The mizguided boy hadn't learnt his lesson. ____________

It was unfortunete that we had to change our plans. ____________

There was an unplesant smell coming from the kitchen. ____________

I was worried I would dislocait my knee again. ____________

The vitamin tablet will disolv when I place it in water. ____________

I caught a thread on my jumper and it started to unraval. ____________

While my dad was unemploied, he started his own business. ____________

We were in unown territory. ____________

The engineers were careful not to miscalcuelate. ____________

Challenge words

6 Write the word.

unnatural ____________

disinterested ____________

discriminate ____________

disobedient ____________

unnecessary ____________

unfamiliar ____________

disentangle ____________

unconscious ____________

unacceptable ____________

discontinue ____________

7 Hidden words. Find the challenge word.

unfamunfamiliarsyna ____________

diisdiscontinuedicson ____________

siousunconsciousunc ____________

dissdisinterestedested ____________

natuunnaturalunnat ____________

entagdisentangledisent ____________

8 Word clues. Which challenge word matches?

separate ____________

naughty ____________

cease ____________

artificial ____________

9 Complete the sentence.

The poor standard of work was ____________ .

They were unable to ____________ between the two chocolate brands.

Her dog was very ____________ and dug many holes.

We had to ____________ all the knots we made in the rope.

Plurals – s, es

List **1 Write the word.**

stitches ______
lenses ______
sleeves ______
styles ______
stretches ______
weaknesses ______
colleges ______
clashes ______
witnesses ______
diseases ______
approaches ______
reserves ______
routes ______
vegetables ______
magazines ______
influences ______
passages ______
audiences ______
obstacles ______
tissues ______

2 Rewrite the words as plurals.

vegetable ______
stitch ______
weakness ______
influence ______
disease ______
sleeve ______
witness ______
audience ______
lens ______
college ______
tissue ______
clash ______
style ______
approach ______
stretch ______
route ______
passage ______
obstacle ______
reserve ______
magazine ______

3 Chunks. Rearrange the letters to make a list word.

s-yle-st ______
s-sage-pas ______
ea-dis-ses ______
es-ness-weak ______
sh-a-es-cl ______
es-ro-ut ______
ee-ves-sl ______
s-lege-col ______
serve-re-s ______
itch-es-st ______
es-proach-ap ______
es-ness-wit ______
es-veg-ta-bl-e ______
ac-ob-les-st ______

Plurals – s, es

4 Complete each sentence with a list word.

We had to do three different ________________ on each leg before we could run.
It is important to eat five servings of ________________ every day.
I pulled my ________________ down when it started to get cold.
My mum cleaned the ________________ of her glasses with a cloth.
The orchestra was performing to ________________ around the world.
We used all of the ________________ in our house when we had colds.
It is said that rats carry many ________________.
There were many ________________ to overcome on the course.
We were collecting ________________ to cut pictures from.
The biggest ________________ in my life have been my mother and father.

Challenge words

5 Write the word.

businesses ________________
addresses ________________
committees ________________
references ________________
performances ________________
temperatures ________________
certificates ________________
disturbances ________________
catalogues ________________
privileges ________________

6 Word clues. Which challenge word matches?

homes ________________
diplomas ________________
brochures ________________
interruptions ________________
advantages ________________
work places ________________

7 Hidden words. Find the challenge word.

encereferencesreff ________________
aturtemperaturesterm ________________
mmtcommitteesees ________________
anceperformancesperf ________________

8 Complete the sentence.

We are putting on three ________________ of the play.
The nurse taught us to measure our ________________ using a thermometer.
We searched the store ________________ to find the best deal.
My parents serve on many charity ________________.
We had to get five bronze ________________ before we could receive a silver one.

Suffixes – ist

5.17

List **1 Write the word.**

artist ____________________
tourist ____________________
florist ____________________
novelist ____________________
dentist ____________________
cyclist ____________________
cartoonist ____________________
finalist ____________________
soloist ____________________
motorist ____________________
pianist ____________________
journalist ____________________
violinist ____________________
machinist ____________________
vocalist ____________________
guitarist ____________________
botanist ____________________
zoologist ____________________
specialist ____________________
ecologist ____________________

2 Name.

3 Complete these list words.

gu ____________	zo ____________
ec ____________	ca ____________
to ____________	so ____________
pi ____________	mo ____________

4 Chunks. Rearrange the letters to make a list word.

ist-fin-al ____________	or-mot-ist ____________
e-gist-o-col ____________	chin-ma-ist ____________
lin-vi-ist-o ____________	el-nov-ist ____________
an-bot-ist ____________	o-ist-sol ____________
list-cyc ____________	cal-ist-vo ____________
ist-jou-al-rn ____________	nt-ist-de ____________
ar-ist-t ____________	oo-ni-ca-st-rt ____________

Suffixes – ist

5 Underline the spelling mistake. Write the word correctly.

The pianoist played a lovely piece at the recital. __________

The flaurist placed the beautiful flowers in a vase. __________

The artiste painted the scenery at the beach. __________

The tourest took many photos of the Eiffel Tower. __________

After I injured my knee, I had to see a specialest. __________

The cartoonest drew a picture of me as a superhero! __________

My dentast gave me a free toothbrush. __________

The jounalest was ready to ask the celebrity as many questions as possible. __________

Before I was born, my dad was a guitarust in a band. __________

The zoologast fed the crocodiles in front of an audience. __________

Challenge words

6 Write the word.

- receptionist __________
- opportunist __________
- conservationist __________
- archaeologist __________
- psychologist __________
- terrorist __________
- environmentalist __________
- perfectionist __________
- nationalist __________
- traditionalist __________

7 Hidden words. Find the challenge word.

- torsterroristterr __________
- psychpsychologistiist __________
- strattraditionalisttrai __________
- aristarchaeologististtr __________
- pposoopportunistisst __________
- perfscperfectionististp __________

8 Word clues. Which challenge word matches?

a person who likes the old ways __________

secretary __________

therapist __________

9 Another way to say it. Which challenge word could replace the underlined word?

The <u>secretary</u> answered the phone in a professional manner. __________

The <u>scientist</u> discovered a tomb in Egypt. __________

A <u>fighter</u> was responsible for the attack. __________

Everyone said he was a real <u>schemer</u>. __________

Palindromes and portmanteaus

List **1 Write the word.**

madam ______________________
level ______________________
smog ______________________
newscast ______________________
motel ______________________
sagas ______________________
refer ______________________
racecar ______________________
taxicab ______________________
brunch ______________________
redder ______________________
squiggle ______________________
chortle ______________________
rotor ______________________
kayak ______________________
radar ______________________
ginormous ______________________
fortnight ______________________
cheeseburger ______________________
paratrooper ______________________

2 Sort the words.

Palindromes

______________ ______________
______________ ______________
______________ ______________
______________ ______________
______________ ______________

Portmanteau

______________ ______________
______________ ______________
______________ ______________
______________ ______________
______________ ______________
______________ ______________

3 Chunks. Fill in the missing letters.

___hort___ ___ r___f___r
s___ ___as r___d___e___
___ada___ ___ew___ca___t
s___ ___igg___e r___c___c___r
k___y___k l___ve___

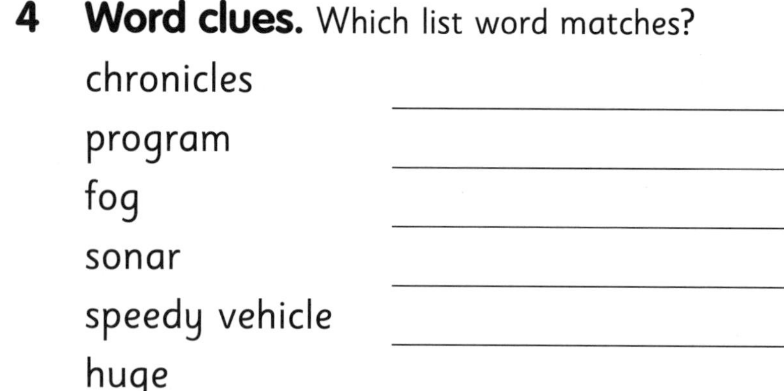

4 Word clues. Which list word matches?

chronicles ______________________
program ______________________
fog ______________________
sonar ______________________
speedy vehicle ______________________
huge ______________________
boat ______________________

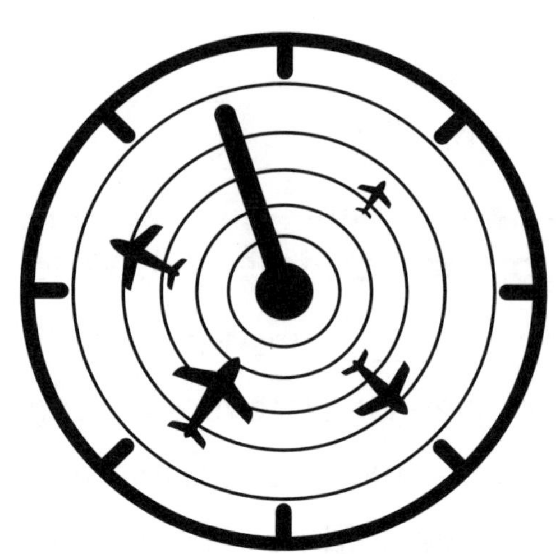

Palindromes and portmanteaus

5 Complete each sentence with a list word.

We stayed overnight in a ________________ .

I had a ________________ and chips for lunch.

Another ship showed up on our ship's ________________ .

I picked the red ________________ to drive on the driving game.

We had people coming over at 11am for a ________________ of bacon and eggs.

The ________________ steered his parachute as best he could.

Our teacher drew a ________________ and we had to turn it into a picture.

My family hired a ________________ and we spent the day paddling.

I had to wait a ________________ for my sister to return from her holiday.

Challenge words

6 Write the word.

rotator ________________

guesstimate ________________

deified ________________

emoticon ________________

cyberspace ________________

reviver ________________

rotavator ________________

simulcast ________________

nanosecond ________________

knowledgebase ________________

7 Hidden words. Find the challenge word.

wkaoyrotavatorvatr ________________

asdjksimulcastcasst ________________

asdrknowledgebasebase ________________

rottarotatortorea ________________

nannonanosecondasink ________________

sdfunareviververyah ________________

timaguesstimatetimg ________________

ieonemoticonemot ________________

defideifiedfied ________________

cyspcyberspaceybsp ________________

8 Another way to say it. Which challenge word could replace the underlined word/s?

Sandra used a <u>smiley face</u> at the end of her text message. ________________

The computer performed the task in a <u>blink of an eye</u>. ________________

Some ancient tribes <u>idolized</u> their kings. ________________

The sporting event was <u>transmitted</u> on television and radio. ________________

They presented their slideshow using <u>the internet</u>. ________________

This number is a <u>rough calculation</u> of the number of people here. ________________

Suffixes – ous

List | **1 Write the word.**

numerous
glorious
meticulous
tedious
ominous
devious
monstrous
victorious
envious
outrageous
religious
marvellous
hazardous
hilarious
vicious
ambitious
indigenous
gracious
courteous
ferocious

2 Write the list words in alphabetical order.

3 Unscramble these list words.

suollevram
osumino
cisfreouo
mnstrouos
dtuosei
cviusio

4 Underline the spelling mistake. Write the word correctly.

I was envyous of my friend's trip to Japan.
Our neighbours have a ferrocious dog.
I have watched that hilerious movie many times.
The villain acted in a deevius way.
There had been a hazerdus chemical spill.
Someone with a glorias voice was singing my favourite song.
Washing the dishes is such a teedious chore.

Suffixes – ous

5 Which word means?

successful ____________ wonderful ____________
funny ____________ native ____________
polite ____________ boring ____________
many ____________ dishonest ____________
dangerous ____________ careful ____________
jealous ____________ fierce ____________

Challenge words

6 Write the word.

suspicious ____________
conscious ____________
surreptitious ____________
harmonious ____________
conscientious ____________
mischievous ____________
righteous ____________
superstitious ____________
advantageous ____________
miscellaneous ____________

7 Word clues. Which challenge word matches?

secretive ____________
assorted ____________
ethical ____________
peaceful ____________
virtuous ____________
helpful ____________

8 Hidden words. Find the challenge word.

icousconsciousssct ____________
ievemischievousmi ____________
supsuperstitiousous ____________
scieconscientioustzc ____________

9 Complete the sentence.

He was a ____________ and hard worker.
My father never walks under ladders as he is ____________.
I thought the story sounded ____________ as the timings didn't match up.
Eating vegetables is ____________ to your health.
The girl was still ____________ after she fell.
The lucky dip bucket was filled with ____________ toys.
His actions helped make the day ____________ and calm.
That guy often gets into trouble because of his ____________ ways.

Plurals – s, ies

List **1 Write the word.**

rallies ________
decoys ________
allies ________
motorways ________
essays ________
volleys ________
energies ________
countries ________
abilities ________
quantities ________
companies ________
difficulties ________
policies ________
discoveries ________
deputies ________
penalties ________
salaries ________
journeys ________
assemblies ________
identities ________

2 Make the words plural.

quantity ________
rally ________
energy ________
assembly ________
motorway ________
essay ________
ally ________
difficulty ________
salary ________
decoy ________
company ________
deputy ________
identity ________
discovery ________
ability ________
policy ________
volley ________
penalty ________
journey ________
country ________

3 Complete these words with *ys* or *ies*.

rall________
all________
casualt________
journe________
volle________
deco________
countr________
motorwa________
identit________
polic________
energ________
deput________
assembl________
penalt________
compan________
discover________

4 Match the clue with the list word.

payments ________
trips ________
amounts ________
lands ________
businesses ________
punishments ________
friends ________
highways ________
hardships ________

5 Word groups. Which list word matches?

energy, energetic, ______
inabillity, ability, ______
penalise, penalty, ______
assemble, assembled, ______
difficult, difficulty, ______
discover, discovers, ______

rally, rallying, ______
journey, journeyed, ______
ally, allied, ______
volleyed, volley, ______
identify, identity, ______
decoy, decoyed, ______

Challenge words

6 Write the word.

opportunities ______
responsibilities ______
communities ______
universities ______
laboratories ______
casualties ______
similarities ______
attorneys ______
possibilities ______
personalities ______

7 Hidden words. Find the challenge word.

comcommunitiesumu ______
borilaboratoriestesl ______
sssibepossibilitiesilit ______
tiesuniversitiesunves ______
torneyattorneysatto ______
casseucasualitieslitca ______

8 Word clues. Which challenge word matches?

likenesses ______
workshops ______
probabilities ______
lawyers ______

9 Another way to say it. Which challenge word could replace the underlined word?

My brother was choosing between two different colleges. ______
The resemblances between the siblings far outweighed their differences. ______
Her tasks at home included helping with dinner. ______
The two girls had similar characteristics and so got on very well. ______
They had many chances to score a goal. ______
The various neighbourhoods joined together to help each other after the fire. ______

Adding to fer

List **1 Write the word.**

differ ________________
offer ________________
refer ________________
prefer ________________
transfer ________________
infer ________________
confer ________________
defer ________________
suffer ________________
offering ________________
differed ________________
different ________________
difference ________________
referee ________________
preferred ________________
transferred ________________
inferring ________________
conferring ________________
deferred ________________
suffered ________________

2 Sort the words.

Words with suffix *ing*

________________ ________________
________________ ________________

Words with suffix *ed*

________________ ________________
________________ ________________
________________ ________________

Words with suffix *ent*

____

Words with suffix *ee*

____

3 Fill in the missing letters.

o____fe____i____g
tra____s____e____re____
r____f____r
t____ ____ns____er
co____f____r
in____e____ ____ing
di____f____re____
d____fe____r____d
c____ ____fe____rin____

4 Complete each sentence with a list word.

I ________________ red apples to green apples.

Dad didn't follow a recipe, so the meal tasted ________________ each time.

The age ________________ between my sister and me is three years.

The ________________ blew his whistle at the end of the football match.

The price included a free ________________ from the airport to the hotel.

Ben accepted the ________________ to go to his friend's house.

Adding to fer

5 Word building. Add suffixes to build words.

infer –
s ____
ed ____
ing ____

differ –
s ____
ed ____
ing ____

prefer –
s ____
ed ____
ing ____

suffer –
s ____
ed ____
ing ____

offer –
s ____
ed ____
ing ____

transfer –
s ____
ed ____
ing ____

confer –
s ____
ed ____
ing ____

defer –
s ____
ed ____
ing ____

Challenge words

6 Write the word.

referred ____
reference ____
preference ____
referral ____
transference ____
inference ____
inferential ____
conference ____
deference ____
preferential ____

7 Word clues. Which challenge word matches?

politeness ____
interpretation ____
movement ____
meeting ____
favourite ____
favoured ____

8 Hidden words. Find the challenge word.

fereinferentialial ____
encedeferencedef ____
refereferredferr ____
reffreferralrral ____

9 Complete the sentence.

The ____ I used in my project came from an encyclopedia.
We received ____ seating on the plane as we were frequent flyers.
Dad attended a work ____ in another state.
Her ____ skills made it possible for her to work out the answer.
My ____ is for chocolate flavoured ice-cream.
The children showed proper ____ to the elderly people.

Word endings – age, idge

List — **1 Write the word.**

heritage
vintage
bridge
damage
bondage
hostage
storage
manage
package
leakage
drainage
coverage
porridge
savage
voyage
postage
wastage
stoppage
marriage
dosage

2 Sort the words.

age

idge

3 Unscramble these list words.

gobedan
egamad
repogrid
edogsa
ethgreia
avsgae
dgbrei

4 Underline the spelling mistake. Write the correct word.

The network is providing live covrage of the game.
The rain kept me hostege inside all day long.
The postege stamps cost more than I expected.
Leekage from the fuel tanks covered a wide area.
The astronaut hoped to make a voyege to the moon.
My parents recently celebrated twenty years of mariege.
My parents refurbish vintege furniture as a hobby.

Word endings – age, idge

5 Meaning. Which list word means?

someone held prisoner ____________
an amount of medicine ____________
from an older time ____________
not tamed; wild ____________
to direct or control ____________
a breakfast food ____________

Challenge words

6 Write the word.

luggage ____________
garbage ____________
plumage ____________
orphanage ____________
cartilage ____________
advantage ____________
beverage ____________
pilgrimage ____________
rummage ____________
sewerage ____________

7 Hidden words. Find the challenge word.

garbaggarbageaget ____________
asdtrsewerageauitba ____________
sdafluggageoiasy ____________
orpahorphanageasoidh ____________
aseugrummageaosiyd ____________
poaopilgrimageorpah ____________

8 Word clues. Which challenge word matches?

feathers ____________
waste ____________
search ____________
drainage ____________
baggage ____________

9 Complete the sentence.

We checked in our ____________ at the airport.
We threw the ____________ into the bin.
The ____________ pipe had cracked and the smell was awful.
Some children have to live in an ____________.
Male peacocks have beautifully coloured ____________.
A cool ____________ is refreshing on a hot day.
The other team had the ____________ of being tall.
Your nose is made from ____________, not bone.

Suffixes – ment, ship, hood, dom

List — **1 Write the word.**

stardom ______
motherhood ______
settlement ______
chiefdom ______
workmanship ______
wisdom ______
kingdom ______
assessment ______
priesthood ______
replacement ______
attachment ______
engagement ______
achievement ______
management ______
assignment ______
likelihood ______
abandonment ______
knighthood ______
measurement ______
citizenship ______

2 Put the letters in the right order.

ment-ace-re-pl ______
li-hood-like ______
ieve-ment-ach ______
dom-chief ______
t-hood-knigh ______
ment-en-gage ______
sure-ment-mea ______
hood-er-moth ______
hood-st-prie ______

3 Sort the words.

ment

______ ______
______ ______
______ ______
______ ______
______ ______

ship

______ ______

hood

______ ______
______ ______

dom

______ ______
______ ______

4 Meaning. Which list word means?

the act of achieving ______

an area ruled by a chief ______

a meeting with someone at a certain time ______

the specific size of something ______

a judgement or evaluation ______

a person that takes the position of another ______

an area ruled by a king ______

Suffixes – ment, ship, hood, dom

5 Match the clue with the list word.

the status of belonging to a certain country c ______
skill with which a product is made w ______
experience, knowledge and good judgement w ______
a bond of fondness or loyalty to something a ______
to leave something without warning a ______
a task, usually with a deadline a ______
person or persons in charge of business m ______
celebrity status s ______

Challenge words

6 Write the word.

environment ______
recruitment ______
embarrassment ______
apprenticeship ______
announcement ______
disappointment ______
encouragement ______
imprisonment ______
advertisement ______
companionship ______

7 Word clues. Which challenge word matches?

captivity ______
hiring ______
broadcast ______
shame ______
commercial ______
inspiration ______

8 Hidden words. Find the challenge word.

evntenvironmentenrim ______
compacompanionshipin ______
diadisappointmentppe ______
shipapprenticeshipapp ______

9 Complete the sentence.

It caused her great ______ when she realised she had called him the wrong name.

My mum went to a ______ agency to find a new job.

I am always grateful for the ______ my parents give me.

It was a big ______ to hear that my favourite band would not tour.

I had seen an ______ for a new show I wanted to watch.

We always recycle to help protect the ______.

Vowel sounds

List | **1 Write the word.**

brigade ____________________
volume ____________________
athlete ____________________
conclude ____________________
stampede ____________________
accuse ____________________
costume ____________________
operate ____________________
cascade ____________________
control ____________________
hurricane ____________________
recognise ____________________
calculate ____________________
indicate ____________________
crocodile ____________________
commute ____________________
appetite ____________________
casserole ____________________
paradise ____________________
absolute ____________________

2 Complete these words.

cos__________
app__________
stam__________
croc__________
ath__________
vol__________
conc__________
brig__________

3 Fill in the missing letters.

i___d___ca___ ___
a___ ___u___e
___b___ ___l___t___
c___m___ut___
o___ ___r___t___
c___ ___s___r___ ___e
___ri___ ___de
r___cog ___ ___se

4 Name.

5 Complete each sentence with a list word.

The elephants began to ______________, knocking down trees as they went.

My parents told me to turn down the ______________ of my music.

Her hair was so long that it would ______________ down her back.

My favourite animal at the wildlife park was the ______________ because I liked its big teeth.

I loved my ______________ for the party so much I wanted to wear it all the time.

In our house, we each have an hour in which we are in ______________ of the TV.

My grandma wasn't feeling well, so we took her a beef ______________ for dinner.

I tried to ______________ the price before the sales assistant did.

The ______________ trained daily in the hope of making the Olympic team.

Challenge words

6 Write the word.

pronounce ______________

balustrade ______________

cellophane ______________

palindrome ______________

electrocute ______________

scrutinise ______________

demonstrate ______________

diagnose ______________

pantomime ______________

insecticide ______________

7 Hidden words. Find the challenge word.

asrdemonstrateasduih ______________

asdfinsecticideoaih ______________

asdrbalustradeoiyba ______________

crysscrutiniseisse ______________

asdtpantomimeitvou ______________

prropronounceaosuih ______________

srcypalindromeproza ______________

asdeeelectrocuteouasg ______________

ophacellophanehace ______________

adaidiagnoseeose ______________

8 Another way to say it. Which challenge word could replace the underlined word?

I held onto the <u>handrail</u> on the stairs to help my balance. ______________

I watched my brother <u>perform</u> his karate skills. ______________

The mechanic had to look under the bonnet to <u>determine</u> the problem. ______________

Dad sprayed <u>pesticide</u> around our house at the start of spring. ______________

People often <u>say</u> my name incorrectly. ______________

Suffixes – tion, sion, cian

List **1 Write the word.**

action ____
protection ____
election ____
direction ____
connection ____
collection ____
relation ____
discussion ____
television ____
operation ____
conclusion ____
expansion ____
physician ____
admission ____
situation ____
population ____
attention ____
application ____
celebration ____
introduction ____

2 Sort the words.

tion

____ ____
____ ____
____ ____
____ ____
____ ____
____ ____
____ ____

sion

____ ____
____ ____
____ ____

cian

____

3 Complete these words with *tion, sion* or *cian*.

direc____	celebra____
expan____	physi____
popula____	protec____
discus____	conclu____

4 Underline the spelling mistake. Write the word correctly.

The director called for acshun and we began the scene. ____
My introduccian to karate was an enjoyable experience. ____
We had a bad conection on the phone. ____
Driving on a slippery road can lead to a dangerous situasion. ____
I paid close attensian to the football game and was still unsure of the end score. ____
The admition fee is $5 each and has to be paid at the front gate. ____

Suffixes – tion, sion, cian

5 Meaning. Which list word means?

something made larger ____________
a doctor of medicine ____________
something planned in order to honour someone ____________
the process of choosing a leader by voting ____________
the preface to a book ____________
the people who live in an area ____________
control or guidance ____________
a group of things of the same type ____________

Challenge words

6 Write the word.

opposition ____________
competition ____________
concession ____________
contribution ____________
communication ____________
institution ____________
association ____________
organisation ____________
tactician ____________
mathematician ____________

7 Word clues. Which challenge word matches?

the act of disagreeing ____________
the act of allowing something ____________
a large organisation ____________
payment or effort ____________
a planner ____________
a partnership ____________

8 Complete the sentence.

My parents made a large ____________ to the fundraiser.
The ____________ was capable of working out long and complex sums.
There were eight teams in my basketball ____________.
A school is an ____________ of learning.
Her main ____________ was Tim, as he was also excellent at debating.
The government is in ____________ with everybody who wants to talk.

Digraphs – ch

List

1 Write the word.

List	Write the word
aching	
attached	
detach	
chutney	
charcoal	
choral	
chrome	
cache	
anchovy	
chimpanzee	
brooch	
chemical	
cockroach	
bachelor	
cheque	
chariot	
echidna	
arachnid	
chiffon	
chameleon	

2 Sort the words.

ch as a 'k' sound

ch as a 'ch' sound

ch as a 'sh' sound

3 Unscramble these list words.

eathdc

ocbralhe

aclrohac

otcahir

echca

ehipcemnza

4 Name.

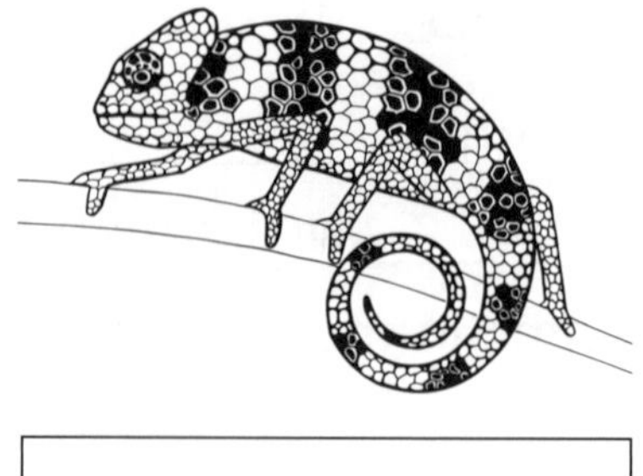

5 Word clues. Which list word matches?

spicy sauce or relish

c ____________________

small, spiky mammal

e ____________________

sung by a choir

c ____________________

small fish

a ____________________

jewellery with a clasp or pin

b ____________________

a spider

a ____________________

a type of metal

c ____________________

used to pay for something

c ____________________

sore

a ____________________

a type of fabric

c ____________________

Challenge words

6 Write the word.

archaic ____________________

epoch ____________________

choreograph ____________________

charisma ____________________

chauffeur ____________________

cholesterol ____________________

chamomile ____________________

avalanche ____________________

chiropractor ____________________

crochet ____________________

7 Word clues. Which challenge word matches?

era ____________________

needlework ____________________

charm ____________________

driver ____________________

landslide ____________________

ancient ____________________

8 Hidden words. Find the challenge word.

chirchiropractorpra ____________________

gapchoreographap ____________________

terocholesterolloes ____________________

9 Complete the sentence.

She drank ________________ tea to help her upset stomach.

The ________________ drove us in a limousine.

I helped my sister to ________________ some dance moves for the show.

Dad sees a ________________ to help his sore back.

The invention of the telephone started an important ________________ in communication.

Tricky words

List

1 Write the word.

nervous ______
width ______
neither ______
similar ______
beginning ______
calendar ______
twelfth ______
variety ______
courage ______
people ______
definite ______
naturally ______
nuisance ______
government ______
yacht ______
harass ______
profession ______
original ______
recommend ______
persuade ______

2 Name.

3 Unscramble these list words.

terenih ______
tnemnrevog ______
vnseuor ______
yllarutan ______
mrdnecemo ______
etinifed ______
gngnbneii ______

4 Put the syllables back together.

ern-ment-gov ______
vous-ner ______
mend-om-rec ______
ther-nei ______
rass-ha ______
age-cour ______

ning-gin-be ______
i-o-nal-rig ______
ple-peo ______
nite-def-i ______
suade-per ______
i-sim-lar ______

Tricky words

5 Complete each sentence with a list word.

I can easily swim the ______________ of the pool, but I struggle with the length.

I have ______________ curly hair, but I can make it straight using a straightener.

My birthday was on the ______________ of October.

I loved the book from ______________ to end.

The venue was filled with excited ______________ waiting for the show to begin.

The shop has a ______________ of different styles.

Doctors ______________ getting regular exercise.

The friends look very ______________, even though they aren't related.

Challenge words

6 Write the word.

guarantee	______________
occurred	______________
ceremony	______________
restaurant	______________
parallel	______________
parliament	______________
immediately	______________
temporary	______________
unanimous	______________
pronunciation	______________

7 Hidden words. Find the challenge word.

papapparallelllep	______________
sibunanimousunamus	______________
asdupronunciationposn	______________
asdutemporaryzsdn	______________
asrdparliamentasdoib	______________
monyceremonyasdu	______________

8 Word clues. Which challenge word matches?

government	______________
makeshift	______________
united	______________
happened	______________

9 Another way to say it. Which challenge word could replace the underlined word?

We ordered 3 different courses at the fancy <u>cafeteria</u>. ______________

The lines run <u>next</u> to one another. ______________

The athletes were honoured at a special <u>function</u>. ______________

They could give us no <u>assurance</u> that the plan would work. ______________

Once mum called us, we <u>promptly</u> went home. ______________

Vowel digraphs – oo, ou

List **1 Write the word.**

igloo ____________
baboon ____________
lagoon ____________
snooze ____________
loosen ____________
wound ____________
should ____________
hooray ____________
through ____________
shampoo ____________
cocoon ____________
groove ____________
troupe ____________
noodle ____________
oozing ____________
coupon ____________
cuckoo ____________
routine ____________
ballooned ____________
boomerang ____________

2 Sort the words.

Words with *oo*

____________ ____________
____________ ____________
____________ ____________
____________ ____________
____________ ____________
____________ ____________
____________ ____________

Words with *ou*

____________ ____________
____________ ____________
____________ ____________

3 Complete the words using *oo* or *ou*.

igl________ coc________n
bab________n gr________ve
lag________n tr________pe
sn________ze n________dle
l________sen ________zing
w________nd c________pon
sh________ld ball________ned

4 Put the letters in the right order.

ou-pe-tr ____________
ing-ooz ____________
nd-wou ____________
oo-shamp ____________
oon-lag ____________
oo-dle-n ____________
sn-ze-oo ____________
oo-gr-ve ____________
tine-rou ____________
oon-ball-ed ____________
oon-bab ____________
ang-er-boom ____________
ray-hoo ____________
oo-co-n-c ____________

Vowel digraphs – oo, ou

5 Underline the spelling mistake. Write the correct word.

We walked thru the park to get to the swimming pool. ____________

The cucoo clock chimed twelve times at midday. ____________

I always hit the snoze button when my alarm goes off for school. ____________

The babone liked to eat fruit. ____________

Dad loves Asian food, especially the noudle dishes. ____________

Challenge words

6 Write the word.

tattoo ____________

harpoon ____________

mongoose ____________

typhoon ____________

hooligan ____________

schooner ____________

cockatoo ____________

acoustics ____________

souvenir ____________

bassoon ____________

7 Hidden words. Find the challenge word.

typhntyphoonsiahd ____________

sdfyhooliganihuasa ____________

asdfftattooasdh ____________

asdtmongooseasdiha ____________

asdrschoonerasdiobh ____________

asdrgrsouvenirasdh ____________

8 Word clues. Which challenge word matches?

sounds ____________

cyclone ____________

bird ____________

boat ____________

9 Complete the sentence.

The ____________ squawked loudly as it flew by.

The ____________ struck the whale as it surfaced.

The hall had wonderful ____________ that made listening to music special.

She brought me back a ____________ from her trip.

We sailed in the harbour on a ____________.

The ____________ is a large woodwind instrument.

The dancer had a tribal ____________ on his arm.

The ____________ killed the poisonous snake.

Consonant sounds – wh, gh, ph

List

1 Write the word.

awhile ______
aghast ______
wharf ______
whiten ______
graphic ______
whistles ______
everywhere ______
whereby ______
whisker ______
whirlpool ______
whinge ______
cartwheel ______
wheedle ______
pheasant ______
ghetto ______
somewhat ______
phantom ______
somewhere ______
headphones ______
geography ______

3 Fill in the missing letters.

s___ ___ ewh___t
w___e___d___e
ge___ ___r___ph___
___e___ ___ pho___ ___s
g___et___ ___
w___ ___ te___
c___rt___he___l
___han___ om
w___e___e___y

2 Sort the words.

wh

______ ______
______ ______
______ ______
______ ______
______ ______
______ ______
______ ______

gh

______ ______

ph

______ ______
______ ______
______ ______

4 Complete each sentence with a list word.

I wore my ______ to listen to music on the bus.

My grandfather had one white ______ on his chin.

It's dangerous to swim near the ______ in the lake.

We looked ______ to find the perfect present for my grandmother.

She taught me how to ______ on the grass.

I asked them to wait ______ because I was busy.

Consonant sounds – wh, gh, ph

5 Meaning. Which list word means?

a large bird with a long tail and bright feathers ______________

to try to persuade or influence by flattery ______________

something that seems real but is not ______________

water turning rapidly about a centre and pulling downward ______________

the science of the earth's surface and all life on it ______________

described clearly and vividly ______________

filled with alarm or horror ______________

an area where people live because they are poor or discriminated against ______________

Challenge words

6 Write the word.

lymph ______________

decipher ______________

metaphor ______________

homophone ______________

emphasise ______________

cenotaph ______________

periphery ______________

asphalt ______________

hieroglyphics ______________

claustrophobia ______________

7 Word clues. Which challenge word matches?

perimeter ______________

ancient writing ______________

decode ______________

simile ______________

monument ______________

bitumen ______________

8 Hidden words. Find the challenge word.

phlylymphymyl ______________

ohmhomophoneph ______________

mphemphasiseph ______________

9 Complete the sentence.

I went to the doctor because my ______________ glands were swollen.

He used many descriptive words to ______________ the beauty of what he saw.

The archaeologists discovered ______________ on the wall of the tomb.

Tim had to ______________ the code to know where to meet his friend.

My little brother was scared and stood on the ______________ of the group.

The ______________ got very hot in the middle of summer.

Suffixes – ance, ence

List **1 Write the word.**

distance __________
absence __________
existence __________
offence __________
silence __________
entrance __________
elegance __________
allowance __________
evidence __________
violence __________
appearance __________
arrogance __________
difference __________
brilliance __________
importance __________
obedience __________
patience __________
audience __________
excellence __________
resistance __________

2 Sort the words.

ance

__________ __________
__________ __________
__________ __________
__________ __________
__________ __________

ence

__________ __________
__________ __________
__________ __________
__________ __________
__________ __________
__________ __________

3 Complete these words with *ance* or *ence*.

obedi________ evid________
off________ excell________
import________ sil________
brilli________ dist________
allow________ arrog________

4 Match the clue with the list word.

a doorway e________
people who watch a show a________
refinement, taste and grace e________
time away a________
actions that can harm or damage v________
the ability to spend time on a difficult task p________
opposing power of one force against another r________
not the same d________
being alive or real e________

Suffixes – ance, ence

5 Word clues. Which list word matches?

extreme brightness ______
muteness ______
fighting ______
compliance ______
length ______
defiance ______
looks ______
crowd ______
contrast ______
perfection ______
proof ______
crime ______

Challenge words

6 Write the word.

acceptance ______
interference ______
inheritance ______
innocence ______
magnificence ______
endurance ______
fragrance ______
ignorance ______
annoyance ______
intelligence ______

7 Hidden words. Find the challenge word.

asdeenduranceasiodh ______
sfjoeignoranceasuha ______
mgnimagnificenceaso ______
innainnocenceasoidh ______
nanannoyancesence ______
asfrintelligenceasdoih ______

8 Word clues. Which challenge word matches?

legacy ______
cleverness ______
approval ______
scent ______

9 Another way to say it. Which challenge word could replace the underlined word?

They were angered by my <u>intervention</u> in the matter. ______
I felt <u>displeasure</u> when he interrupted me for the third time. ______
The athlete's <u>stamina</u> in the marathon was unbelievable. ______
The house was filled with the <u>perfume</u> of roses. ______
They were awestruck by the <u>splendour</u> of the sunset. ______
My <u>heirloom</u> from my grandmother was her beautiful sapphire ring. ______

Eponyms

List

atlas
watt
volt
America
mentor
Tuesday
volcano
January
Saturday
python
martial
cardigan
sandwich
boycott
cannibal
vandal
marmalade
saxophone
diesel
Wednesday

1 Write the word.

2 Fill in the missing syllables.

Sat-__________-day
__________-wich
mar-__________-lade
__________-las
vol-__________-no
Tues-__________

3 Name.

4 Unscramble these list words.

lmmadaear __________
ramAcei __________
abcnailn __________
olvt __________
ldnava __________
tbotoyc __________
rotnem __________
wtat __________
elsdei __________
yadsendeW __________
nohtyp __________
sdeauyT __________

Eponyms

5 Underline the spelling mistake. Write the correct word.

The volcanoe erupted and hot lava flowed out. ____________

I brought my cardigen as it was getting cool. ____________

The pithon curled around the tree. ____________

I had orange marmalaid with cream on my scones. ____________

I usually have a cheese sanwicth for lunch. ____________

Janury is the first month of the Roman calendar. ____________

I found Africa in the atlass. ____________

On Saterday my brother and I play soccer. ____________

Challenge words

6 Write the word.

Cartesian ____________

Braille ____________

algorithm ____________

guillotine ____________

mesmerise ____________

silhouette ____________

Fahrenheit ____________

jacuzzi ____________

pasteurise ____________

herculean ____________

7 Hidden words. Find the challenge word.

zzjajacuzziawdg ____________

asdtaguillotineasuihb ____________

asdtapasteuriseasdouih ____________

asdfihcartesianasduoh ____________

asdrgsilhouetteasdoiha ____________

adasdmesmeriseasodugh ____________

8 Word clues. Which challenge word matches?

temperature ____________

printing ____________

shadow ____________

fascinate ____________

9 Complete the sentence.

Our teacher taught us an ____________ to work out the area of a triangle.

The dairy will ____________ your milk before they sell it you.

Americans measure the temperature using the ____________ scale.

____________ is a special form of writing that allows blind people to read.

Cleaning up our whole house would be a ____________ task.

I saw my friend's ____________ through the curtains before I opened the door.

Suffixes – ly

List **1 Write the word.**

clearly ____________
simply ____________
largely ____________
quietly ____________
loosely ____________
daily ____________
totally ____________
formerly ____________
ideally ____________
hastily ____________
completely ____________
possibly ____________
basically ____________
enormously ____________
hurriedly ____________
privately ____________
beautifully ____________
thoroughly ____________
primarily ____________
legally ____________

2 Write the list words in alphabetical order.

____________ ____________
____________ ____________
____________ ____________
____________ ____________
____________ ____________
____________ ____________
____________ ____________
____________ ____________
____________ ____________
____________ ____________

3 Fill in the missing syllables.

thor-__________-ly e-__________-mous-ly
i-de-al-__________ hur-__________-ly
leg-al-__________ pri-mar-i-__________
ba-si-__________-ly to-__________-ly
loose-__________ qui-__________-ly
poss-__________-bly pri-__________-ly

4 Complete each sentence with a list word.

Her hair hung ____________ on her shoulders.
I wanted to talk to my friend ____________ because I had a secret to tell her.
The pathway was ____________ covered in water.
I eat three pieces of fruit ____________.
Our football team was ____________ known as the Roosters, but now we are the Ravens.
The venue was decorated ____________ and looked amazing.
We walked ____________ to our appointment so as not to be late.

Suffixes – ly

5 In a group. Write the list word that belongs in each group.

ideal, ideals, ______________________

legal, illegal, ______________________

haste, hasten, ______________________

hourly, monthly, ______________________

beauty, beautiful, ______________________

simple, simplify, ______________________

Challenge words

6 Write the word.

particularly ______________________

especially ______________________

deliberately ______________________

surprisingly ______________________

approximately ______________________

remarkably ______________________

presumably ______________________

temporarily ______________________

automatically ______________________

occasionally ______________________

7 Word clues. Which challenge word matches?

without thinking ______________________

now and then ______________________

on purpose ______________________

for a short time ______________________

shockingly ______________________

about ______________________

8 Hidden words. Find the challenge word.

pecialespeciallyasdua ________________

beratdeliberatelyasdo ________________

llyoccasionallyasdbp ________________

adaapproximatelyasdi ________________

9 Complete the sentence.

I love ice-cream, ______________________ chocolate ice-cream.

The door to the shop opened ______________________.

That's not fair! She did that ______________________ to annoy me.

I am ______________________ two years older than him.

The exhibit was ______________________ closed due to maintenance.

Dad ______________________ lets us go alone.

You have everything you need, ______________________?

Spelling patterns – que

List

cheque
plaque
mosque
bouquet
unique
opaque
antique
lacquer
conquer
queue
macaque
oblique
boutique
conqueror
grotesque
mystique
technique
brusque
physique
racquet

1 Write the word.

2 Chunks. Rearrange the letters in the right order.

mo-que-s
q-un-ue-i
br-que-us
q-con-uer
e-que-ch
si-ue-phy-q
es-gro-que-t
que-a-op
que-pla
ue-que
que-lac-r

3 In a group. Write the list word that belongs in each group.

church, temple,
monkey, ape,
flower, bunch,
diagonal, slanting,
original, special,
ugly, hideous,

4 Meaning. Which list word means?

a small shop, usually selling clothes
the particular method of doing something
an aura of mystery that surrounds certain people or activities
a liquid used on wood to protect and make it shiny.
being the only one of its type
a flat plate or tablet with writing on it
not able to be seen through

Spelling patterns – que

5 Underline the spelling mistake. Write the correct word.

Grandma gave me a check for $20 for my birthday. ______________

I chose a pink racket to play tennis with on Saturday. ______________

I made a boucket of flowers from the plants in our garden. ______________

My storeroom is always dark because of the opaike window. ______________

I have learnt the techniqe of icing cupcakes. ______________

The cue at the bakery went all the way around the block. ______________

My dad likes to lacker the wooden deck outside once a year. ______________

My team received a placqe for winning the tournament. ______________

Challenge words

6 Write the word.

critique ______________

marquee ______________

etiquette ______________

masquerade ______________

clique ______________

croquette ______________

statuesque ______________

tourniquet ______________

discotheque ______________

marquetry ______________

7 Word clues. Which challenge word matches?

manners ______________

canopy ______________

masked party ______________

fried food ______________

wooden floor ______________

8 Hidden words. Find the challenge word.

tqdidiscothequeas ______________

licilcliquequeli ______________

nqutourniquetquat ______________

crottcroquetteettec ______________

sttstatuesqueesqu ______________

9 Complete the sentence.

The ______________ floor contained various colours and types of wood.

We set up a ______________ in the backyard in case it rained.

I was having a ______________ party where everyone had to wear a mask.

Having good manners is an important part of ______________.

The author was pleased with the glowing ______________ of his new novel.

The nurse used a ______________ to stop my leg bleeding.

We are excited about the ______________ at school on Friday.

The girls formed a ______________ and wouldn't be friends with anyone else.

Word building

List | **1 Write the word.**

flat ____________
flatter ____________
flattest ____________
flatten ____________
flattened ____________
reside ____________
residing ____________
resided ____________
resident ____________
residential ____________
simple ____________
simply ____________
simplify ____________
simplest ____________
simplification ____________
horror ____________
horrible ____________
horrify ____________
horrifying ____________
horrified ____________

2 Write the list words in alphabetical order.

3 Fill in the missing letters.

s___mpli___ ___cati___ ___
fl___ ___te___t
s___m___le___t
re___i___i___g
___im___ ___y
re___ ___d___ ___
h___rr___f___
re___ ___de

4 Complete each sentence with a list word.

The dress that my sister wore was ____________ and elegant.
I watched in ____________ as the car drove over my football.
I had to ____________ the instructions so my little brother could understand them.
As I was a ____________ of the building, I was required at the meeting.
He ____________ the sandcastle with his foot.
The price of petrol always seems to ____________ my mother.
The speed limit in the ____________ zone is lower to keep people safe.

Word building

5 Word building. Add suffixes to build words.

flat –
er ______
est ______
en ______
ened ______
reside –
ing ______
ed ______
ent ______
ntial ______

simple –
y ______
ify ______
st ______
ification ______
horror –
ible ______
ify ______
ifying ______
ified ______

Challenge words

6 Write the word.

benefit ______
benefited ______
benefiting ______
beneficial ______
beneficiary ______
receive ______
receiving ______
received ______
reception ______
receipt ______

7 Hidden words. Find the challenge word.

aduybenefitingting ______
wiohareceptionrece ______
asdrbenefitedaosidh ______
asdasreceiveasdioh ______
asdasbeneficiaryasldbn ______
asdreceivingasodug ______

8 Unravel these challenge words.

fbingeneti ______
deviecer ______
neeitfb ______
noitpecer ______

9 Complete the sentence.

I ______ my pocket money once I had cleaned my room.
Exercising regularly will ______ your heart.
The shop assistant handed me a ______ for the items I had purchased.
I was excited to be ______ my award at assembly.
I could see how much my little brother was ______ from his swimming lessons.
We checked into the hotel at ______.

Loan words

List	1 Write the word.
café	____________
pasta	____________
ballet	____________
studio	____________
gelato	____________
genre	____________
opera	____________
pizza	____________
mousse	____________
croissant	____________
cliché	____________
sauté	____________
macaroni	____________
soprano	____________
sabotage	____________
brunette	____________
rapport	____________
dossier	____________
scenario	____________
baguette	____________

2 Fill in the missing syllables.

mac-a-ro-________

__________-la-to

bru-__________

__________-er-a

bal-__________

__________-port

so-__________-o

gen-__________

3 Name.

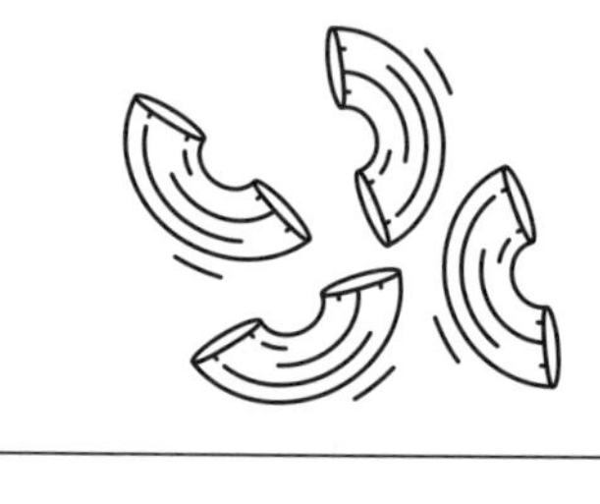

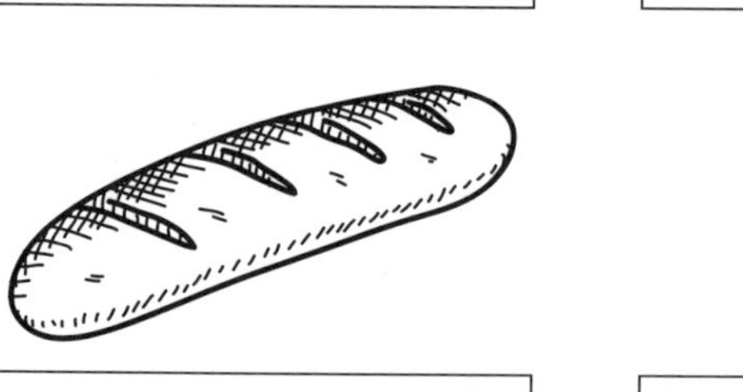

4 Unscramble these list words.

acraomin	____________	droesis	____________
étuas	____________	logeta	____________
doutis	____________	zapiz	____________
ponosar	____________	prtapro	____________
stapa	____________	otbagase	____________
uebteagt	____________	oiranecs	____________

Loan words

5 Match the clue with the list word.

a person with brown hair b ____________
a category of film, writing, music, etc. g ____________
a play that is entirely sung o ____________
dough base with tomato and cheese p ____________
an expression that is overused c ____________
a form of dance b ____________
to fry lightly in oil s ____________
a place to eat and drink coffee c ____________
a long, thin loaf of bread b ____________
the workshop of an artist s ____________
Italian ice-cream g ____________

Challenge words

6 Write the word.

spaghetti ____________
lasagne ____________
saboteur ____________
entrée ____________
staccato ____________
chauffeur ____________
entrepreneur ____________
restaurateur ____________
extravaganza ____________
reconnaissance ____________

7 Word sort. These words are based on other languages. Put them in the correct list.

Italian	French
s	s
l	e
s	c
e	e
	r
	r

8 Another way to say it. Which challenge word could replace the underlined word?

Our school was putting on a musical <u>spectacular</u>. ____________
First I had a <u>starter</u>, and then I had a main course. ____________
Our <u>driver</u> drove us from our house to the wedding. ____________
We completed our <u>exploration</u> of the camp site before setting up our tent. ____________

Prefixes – anti, circum, extra, semi

5.36

List **1 Write the word.**

semifinal ____________
semicircle ____________
extramural ____________
circumvent ____________
antismoking ____________
antidote ____________
semiformal ____________
antifreeze ____________
antihero ____________
semidarkness ____________
semicolon ____________
semiskilled ____________
antisocial ____________
anticlimax ____________
semiprecious ____________
antislavery ____________
antiseptic ____________
semidetached ____________
antibiotic ____________
circumscribe ____________

3 Fill in the missing syllables.

sem-i-__________-ness
ex-_________-mur-__________
_________-i-cir-__________
sem-____-_________-lon
_________-i-de-tached
sem-i-__________-nal
an-________-he-ro
an-________-smok-_________

2 Sort the words.

anti

____________ ____________
____________ ____________
____________ ____________
____________ ____________
____________ ____________
____________ ____________

circum

____________ ____________

extra

____________ ____________

semi

____________ ____________
____________ ____________
____________ ____________
____________ ____________

4 Meaning. Which list word means?

a substance that stops poison from working ____________

one half of a circle ____________

to find a way around an obstacle ____________

a substance that lowers the freezing point of a liquid such as water ____________

against slavery ____________

a disappointingly weak conclusion to an event ____________

Prefixes – anti, circum, extra, semi

5 Underline the spelling mistake. Write the word correctly.

The antedote to a snake's bite must be administered quickly. ____________

We are playing our football semefinal on the weekend. ____________

The pharmacist told me to take the antebiotc with food. ____________

After I fell over, I cleaned my knee with an anteseptik wipe. ____________

The United Kingdom passed an antislavary law in 1807. ____________

My cousin's wedding was semiformale, so I could wear my new dress. ____________

I didn't want to be anticsocel, so I went and spoke to our guests. ____________

Challenge words

6 Write the word.

antibacterial ____________

circumference ____________

semipermanent ____________

extraordinary ____________

semiconscious ____________

antihistamine ____________

circumnavigate ____________

extraterrestrial ____________

extracurricular ____________

semiautomatic ____________

7 Word clues. Which challenge word matches?

to sail around the world ____________

outside regular school activities ____________

a line around a circle ____________

something to treat allergies ____________

exceptional ____________

sterile ____________

Martian ____________

8 Complete the sentence.

The boy takes part in many ____________ activities after school.

I used a ____________ marker to write my name on the label.

I cleaned the kitchen bench with ____________ wipes.

The football player was ____________ as we took him to hospital.

The superhero in the movie could do many ____________ things.

RULES AND GENERALISATIONS

Prefixes

un, dis, mis	The prefix *un*, *dis* or *mis* to a word turns it into its opposite. wise → *unwise* satisfied → *dissatisfied* fortunate → *misfortunate*
anti, circum, extra, semi	The prefix *anti* means against, like *antibacterial*. The prefix *circum* means around or circling, like *circumnavigate*. The prefix *extra* means beyond or outside, like *extraordinary*. The prefix *semi* means half or partly, like *semiprecious*.

Suffixes

s, ies	If a noun ends in *consonant* + *y*, change the *y* to *i* and add *es*, army → *armies*. If a noun ends in *vowel* + *y*, just add *s*, valley → *valleys*.
ly	If the adjective ends in *consonant* + *y*, change the *y* to *i*, weary → *wearily*. If the adjective ends in *ic*, add *ally*, specific → *specifically*.
ion, ian	Turn verbs that end in *t*, *te*, *s*, *se*, *d* or *de* into nouns by adding *ion*. attract → *attraction* communicate → *communication* collide → *collision* Turn some words that end in *c* or *cs* into nouns by adding *ian*, electric → *electrician*.
ity	Turn words into nouns by adding the suffix *ity*, major → *majority*. If a word ends in *e*, drop the *e*, then add *ity*, pure → *purity*. If a word ends in *le*, change *le* to *il* then add *ity*, flexible → *flexibility*.
ment, ship, hood, dom	Turn some verbs into nouns by adding *ment*, like announce → *announcement*. Turn some words into abstract nouns by adding *ship*, *hood* or *dom*. relation → *relationship* child → *childhood* wise → *wisdom*
ous	If the base word ends in *e*, drop the *e* then add *ous*, adventure → *adventurous*. If the base word ends in *consonant* + *y*, change the *y* to *i* then add *ous*, mystery → *mysterious*.
ive	Turn words into adjectives or nouns by adding *ive*, mass → *massive*. When the base word ends in *e*, drop the e then add *ive*, expense → *expensive*. For words that end in *d* or *de*, change the *d* or *de* to *t* or *s* before adding *ive*. attend → *attentive* expand → *expansive* explode → *explosive*
ist	When *ist* is added to a word, it shows someone does something, art → *artist*. Sometimes you must drop the last letter then add *ist*, piano → *pianist*.
ish	Sometimes *ish* is a suffix that is added to words to form adjectives. In these words, *ish* means somewhat like or having the characteristics of, like *childish*. Some words that have the suffix *ish* show where someone or something comes from. These words start with capital letters, like *Irish*.
ance, ence	Turn some verbs into nouns by adding the suffix *ance*, resist → *resistance*. Turn adjectives that end in ant into nouns by changing ant to *ance*, distant → *distance*. Turn some verbs into nouns by adding the suffix ence, interfere → *interference*. Turn adjectives that end in *ent* into nouns by changing *ent* to *ence*, silent → *silence*.
fy	Turn some nouns into verbs by adding *fy*, liquid → *liquefy*.
ic	Turn some words into adjectives by adding the *ic*, poet → *poetic*.